Sea Urchins

by Lola M. Schaefer

Consulting Editor: Gail Saunders-Smith, Ph.D.

Consultant: Jody Byrum, Science Writer,
SeaWorld Education Department

Pebble Books

an imprint of Capstone Press
Mankato, Minnesota

Pebble Books are published by Capstone Press
818 North Willow Street, Mankato, Minnesota 56001
http://www.capstone-press.com

Library of Congress Cataloging-in-Publication Data
Schaefer, Lola M., 1950–
    Sea urchins/by Lola M. Schaefer.
    p. cm.—(Ocean life)
    Includes bibliographical references (p. 23) and index.
    Summary: In simple words and text, describes the sea urchin.
    ISBN 0-7368-0251-7
    1. Sea urchins—Juvenile literature. [1. Sea urchins.] I. Title. II. Series: Schaefer,
Lola M., 1950–   Ocean life.
QL384.E2S32   1999
593.9′5—dc21

                                                            98-46080
                                                                CIP
                                                                 AC

Note to Parents and Teachers

The Ocean Life series supports national science standards for units on the diversity and unity of life. The series shows that animals have features that help them live in different environments. This book describes and illustrates sea urchins, their homes, and their parts. The photographs support early readers in understanding the text. The repetition of words and phrases helps early readers learn new words. This book also introduces early readers to subject-specific vocabulary words, which are defined in the Words to Know section. Early readers may need assistance to read some words and to use the Table of Contents, Words to Know, Read More, Internet Sites, and Index/Word List sections of the book.

2

Table of Contents

4

Sea urchins are
ocean animals.

6

Some sea urchins live on rocks.

8

Some sea urchins live near seaweed.

mouth

Each sea urchin has
a mouth.

teeth

Each sea urchin has five teeth.

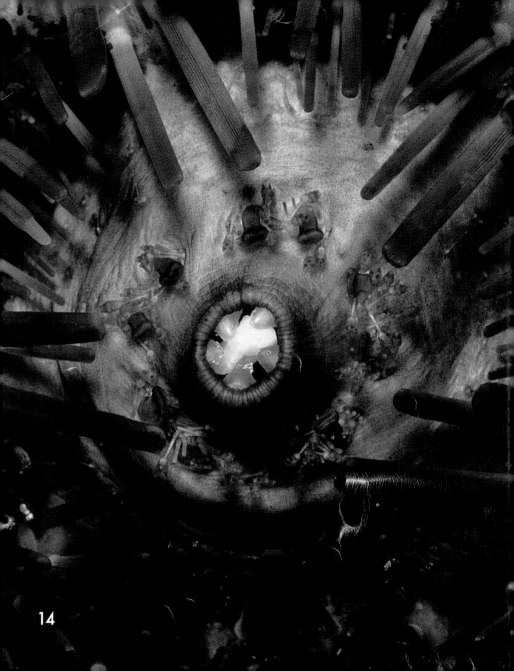

14

Sea urchins grind food with their teeth.

Sea urchins have
sharp spines.

18

Spines hide sea urchins.

Spines protect sea urchins from predators.

Words to Know

grind—to crush something into fine pieces; sea urchins use their teeth to grind food into small parts.

predator—an animal that hunts other animals; sea urchin predators include birds, sea stars, and lobsters.

protect—to guard or keep safe from harm; sea urchins use their sharp spines to protect themselves from predators.

seaweed—a plant that grows in the ocean; sea urchins often eat seaweed.

spine—a sharp, pointed growth on some plants or animals

Read More

Cooper, Jason. *Sea Urchins.* Animals without Bones. Vero Beach, Fla.: Rourke, 1996.

Swartz, Stanley L. *Starfish and Urchins.* Marine Life for Young Readers. Carlsbad, Calif.: Dominie Press, 1997.

Tibbitts, Christiane Kump. *Seashells, Crabs, and Sea Stars.* Young Naturalist Field Guides. Milwaukee: Gareth Stevens, 1998.

Internet Sites

Purple Urchin
http://database.mbl.edu/SPECIMENS/
phylum.taf?function=detail&ID=161

Sea and Sky: Echinoderms
http://www.seasky.org/sea2d.html

Sea Urchins
http://www.umassd.edu/Public/People/KAmaral/
Thesis/SeaUrchins.html

Index/Word List

Word Count: 51
Early-Intervention Level: 9

Editorial Credits
Martha E. Hillman, editor; Steve Christensen, cover designer and illustrator; Kimberly Danger and Sheri Gosewisch, photo researchers

Photo Credits
Brian Parker/Tom Stack & Associates, 12
Chris Huss/The Wildlife Collection, 4
Dembinsky Photo Assoc. Inc./E. R. Degginger, 20
James P. Rowan, 6
Jay Ireland & Georgienne Bradley, 14
Randy Morse/Tom Stack & Associates, 8, 18
Richard Herrmann/The Wildlife Collection, cover
Tammy Peluso/Tom Stack & Associates, 1, 16
Unicorn Stock Photos/Dick Keen, 10